BLACK CHILD, HOLD YOUR HEAD HIGH

WRITTEN BY
JASMINE WALKER, MD FAAP

ILLUSTRATED BY DG

Throughout history, countries have formed colonies. They have taken over the land, people, and resources of other countries. But some fought back when others hurt or enslaved them. This is called a *revolt*.

Other Black people gained freedom from colonial powers.

Some Black people govern their own countries.

Yes, you may be different from other Black people.
But hold your head high, Black child.

Our parents were freed from physical slavery.
Then they suffered financial slavery.

Schools were forced to no longer be separated by color. (This is called *desegregation.*) But some teachers doubted our ability to learn.

You may have been hurt or jailed by some hired to protect and serve.

But you may hold your head high, Black child.

Despite your history, journey, pain, and struggle, you have survived.

You responded to challenges by making your own dance, language, and way of life.

You are creative, musical, strong, and smart.
You may hold your head high, Black child.

Your mind and creativity led to inventions that are the backbone of your country.

Henry T. Sampson, Jr. PhD

Serena Williams

Jackie Robinson

Your quickness to change affects sports, fun, and our way of life.

Bob Marley

Machel Montano

Your mind has led and is leading to many advances in medicine, government, engineering, and science.

Hold your head high, Black child. Hold your head high.

Appendix A: Illustration Descriptions

Page 4: The Haitian Revolution was led by ex-slave Toussaint Louverture and ended in 1804, after thirteen years. Self-liberated slaves fought against French colonial rule in Saint-Domingue, now the sovereign state of Haiti. This is the only slave uprising that led to the founding of a state free from slavery that was ruled by former captives.

Page 5: Ghana gained independence from Britain on March 6, 1957. After it achieved independence, Dr. Kwame Nkrumah became the first elected president of Ghana. Ghana was the first African country to gain independence from European colonial powers.

Page 6: Several countries have leaders of color. One of the richest countries in Africa is Nigeria. Abuja is the capital of Nigeria, and this is an illustration of its senate in session.

Page 8: Sharecropping was an economic system where sharecroppers rented farmable land, supplies, and equipment from farmers, such as plantation owners. The sharecropper gave half of their harvest or proceeds from selling their harvest to the farmer in lieu of rent.

The high prices of rental equipment and supplies required the sharecroppers to buy or rent items via credit with high interest rates. Thus, the sharecroppers could not make enough income to buy their land or start savings accounts. This system led to “wage slavery.”

Appendix A: Illustration Descriptions

Page 9: The U.S. Supreme Court ruling in the Plessy v. Ferguson (1896) case supported systemic racism. This ruling supported "separate but equal" train cars, facilities, services, and schools. It allowed local and state governments to develop laws that separated racial groups and led to legal and social mistreatment of Black Americans.

The Supreme Court overturned that horror in the Brown v. Board of Education (1954) case, where the Court said that separate schools for African American students were "inherently unequal." The process of mixing races in public schools was resisted; sometimes with violence.

Page 10: Sometimes committing crimes results in imprisonment, but sometimes fighting social injustice leads to imprisonment. Martin Luther King, Jr. (a civil rights activist in the United States) and Nelson Mandela (an anti-apartheid revolutionary political leader who served as the first president of South Africa from 1994 to 1999) were both placed in jail.

Page 12: Picture of one traditional dance of Kenya

Page 16: Henry T. Sampson Jr., PhD, is an African American engineer and inventor best known for creating the world's first cell phone.

Page 17: Serena Williams is widely considered one of the greatest tennis players of all time. She is an Olympic gold medalist and the first tennis player to achieve a Career Golden Slam in both singles and doubles.

Appendix A: Illustration Descriptions

Page 17: Jackie Robinson was an American professional baseball player who became the first African American to play in Major League Baseball.

Bob Marley was a Jamaican singer, songwriter, and musician. He is one of the pioneers of reggae music.

Machel Montano was born in Trinidad and Tobago and is a very popular Calypso/Soca artist in the Caribbean.

Page 18: Charles Richard Drew, MD, known as the father of blood banking, pioneered blood preservation techniques. His research focused on the best practices for blood banking (storage) and blood transfusions.

Judge Ketanji Brown Jackson is the first Black woman to serve as a justice on the Supreme Court.

Walter Braithwaite was born in Jamaica and received a degree in engineering in 1966. Braithwaite's team developed computer-aided design/computer-aided manufacturing (CAD/CAM) systems for Boeing. This invention paved the way for airplanes and many other products to be designed entirely through software.

In 1992, Dr. Mae Jemison, a trained physician, became the first Black woman astronaut to go into space.

Dedication

This book is dedicated to my first child, whose birth gave me a new outlook on life and my life goals.

Special Acknowledgments

I would like to acknowledge my sister, Jacinta Turner, who shares my vision of entrepreneurship, and my husband, Ronald Walker Jr., for his support on this journey to authorship.

Author Bio:

Dr. Jasmine Walker was born in Dallas, Texas, to educators Walter and Deborah Turner. She is a graduate of the historically Black university Oakwood University and Loma Linda School of Medicine. She has specialized in pediatrics. Dr. Walker has had the privilege of serving children in California, Botswana, and Guam. She is a Christian author, and since becoming a mother of two, her love for writing has been revived. She loves children and aspires to create more books for them.

Share Your Feedback!

Did you enjoy this book? Please post a review on Amazon to let others know about your experience. Your review will help with getting this book into the hands of more children, and we would love to hear your feedback!

Published by Jasmine Walker
Chicago, Illinois

Library of Congress Control Number: 2022907252

Printed in the United States of America
Paperback ISBN: 979-8-9861361-0-3
Hardcover ISBN: 979-8-9861361-1-0
Electronic Format ISBN ebook: 979-8-9861361-2-7

Editing, Illustrations, Layout, & Book Cover Design
by DG Self-Publishing